Never get lost again

INDEX

I0505477

JORGE CABALLERO

Jorge is a graduate in Advertising and Public Relations from Universidad de Sevilla, Spain. Since 2014 he has worked in the hospitality industry in places like Amsterdam or Mallorca. It has specialized in digital hotel marketing and content creation. He worked as a Content Manager in Park Hyatt Mallorca.

WHAT IS AN INSTAGRAM CAPTION

Not the Typical Book of Copy-Paste Instagram Captions

Captions for your hotel is not the typical book of copy-paste Instagram captions. My idea is to inspire you to produce more creative and original content. Of course, you can copy it if you want it. However, I intend you to have clear guidance and more ideas and examples to produce more content with your style.

Why?

1. Instagram ban plagiarism content

2. More engagement

3. More loyal followers. More future guest

4. Great values for your brand: originality, uniqueness...

What Is an Instagram Caption

According to the tool sociality.io, an Instagram caption is:

"An Instagram caption is a text describing or explaining the image. The right combination of hashtags, mentions, and emojis is an ideal recipe for great captions. Posting a picture is not enough to effectively deliver the message you wanted to convey."

INSTAGRAM TOOLS

To improve photos

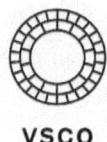
VSCO

To create a unique
Instagram Feed

To manage Instagram Contest

To make Better Instagram Stories

Unfold - Create Stories

To find Better Hashtags

 Focalmark

Send Instagram Users to Your Website

 linktree   Linkin.bio

HOW TO PRODUCE MORE CONTENT FOR YOUR HOTEL WITHOUT LOSE QUALITY

Posting on Instagram Is Not Just a Matter of a Couple of Minutes (Sociality.lo)

1. Invest your time into writing unique captions

2. Plan everything carefully

3. Plan for the whole week, month or year. You will save lots of time

4. Create your own Instagram voice

Here it is my recommendations as a content manager in hotels:

Work With Two or Three Months in Advance

It is recommended to work with enough time. If you want to get the best results for your hotel at Christmas, start creating content last of august. If you want more bookings in summer, start creating content in February or March.

Every Month Has a Special Day

I recommend you to have in mind key days like Halloween, Easter, or Christmas. There are plenty of national days to create content related to it.

Keep It Simple

You don't need the best audiovisual equipment. A smartphone and your brain are more than enough for creating awesome content. Keep in mind that the most important is to have in mind what do you want to communicate.

Planning

A great video or a simple photo needs planning. You should spend more time in have a good planning of what do you want to shot, who, when, and how before or take the camera.

It Is First the Caption or the Photo?

I prefer to work with different captions and try to imagine how it could look like. It is also interesting to spend the day taking photos around your hotel and later work on the caption looking at the pictures.

How To Produce More Content Without Losing Quality?

Before publishing, you should ask yourself how unique is it. How interesting this content for my guest? Keep in mind all the value propositions of your hotel to produce more without losing quality.

Be International but Keep in Mind the Local

In the hospitality industry, it's important to connect with the international guest but also with your local's ones. You should know as much as you can about your city and local events. It helps you a lot to create more.

SAVE THE DATE AND CREATE AWESOME CONTENT

....

› Keep in mind key days it's a great way to create constant content for your hotel. Check the special days in your destination and work with enough time.

› In the hospitality industry, you have to create content following the most important seasons in your destination.

January

- National Spaghetti Day History
- National Popcorn Day
- National Hug Day
- National Hot Chocolate Day
- Martin Luther King Day

February

- National signing day
- World Cancer Day
- Super Bowl
- National Pizza Day
- Chinese New Year
- World Radio Day

- Valentine's Day
- National Drink Wine Day
- National Love Your Pet Day
- National Margarita Day

March

- Zero Discrimination Day
- Employee Appreciation Day
- International Women's Day
- National Napping Day
- World Sleep Day
- Saint Patrick's Day
- International Day Of Happiness
- World Water Day
- National Puppy Day
- International Waffle Day
- Earth Hour Day

April

- Holi
- National Burrito Day
- Easter
- National Beer Day
- National Walking Day
- World Health Day
- National Pet Day
- Ramadan

- Bicycle Day
- Earth Day
- International Jazz Day

May

- Free Comic Book Day
- Mother's Day
- National Wine Day
- National Burger Day
- National Biscuit Day
- Memorial Day

June

- World Bicycle Day
- National Cheese Day
- National Donut Day
- World Environment Day
- Flag Day
- International Picnic Day
- National Flip Flop Day
- Start of Summer
- National Martini Day
- Father's Day
- International Yoga Day
- National Selfie Day
- World Music Day

July

- Canada Day
- Independence Day
- International Kissing Day
- World Chocolate Day
- National Sugar Day
- National Piña Colada Day
- National French Fry Day
- World Emoji Day
- National Ice Cream Day
- National Hot Day
- International Self Care Day
- National Tequila Day
- National Lasagna Day
- National Cheesecake Day
- National Avocado Day

August

- National Ice Cream Sandwich Day
- National Watermelon Day
- International Cat Day
- Book Lovers Day
- National Lazy Day
- National Relaxation Day

September

- International Bacon Day
- National Cheese Pizza Day
- Read A Book Day
- Patriot Day
- Constitution Day
- National Cheeseburger Day
- Oktoberfest (Start)
- National Pepperoni Pizza Day
- International Day of Peace
- Start of Fall (Autumnal Equinox)
- National Pancake Day
- National Chocolate Milk Day
- World Tourism Day
- National Coffee Day
- International Podcast Day
- World Maritime Day

October

- World Smile Day
- World Vegetarian Day
- National Taco Day
- World Egg Day
- National Pasta Day
- National Pumpkin Day
- Halloween
- World Cities Day

November

- Veterans Day
- National Pickle Day
- National Fast Food Day
- National Take A Hike Day
- Thanksgiving Day
- Black Friday
- National Cake Day
- National French Toast Day
- Cyber Monday
- Givings Tuesday

December

- National Cookie Day
- International Volunteer Day
- Saint Nicholas Day
- Start of Winter
- Christmas
- Boxing Day
- St John

CHRISTMAS TIME

....

Random

› Happy Holidays from the team of *@nameofyourhotel* 🌲 Enjoy the festive season with your loved ones! *#lovelytime*

› Time for giving ❄ Share your wish with every Christmas postcard that you can find at reception. *#TimeforGiving #FestiveSeason #ChristmasWishes*

› The festive season is closer than ever at *@nameofyourhotel #TimeforGiving #FestiveSeason #ChristmasWishes*

› *Gift wellness this holiday season. Spa gift voucher available at @nameofyourwebsite. #GiftWellness #HolidaySeason #HotelSpa*

› *Christmas is not a time nor a season, but a state of mind. May this one be one to remember! #ChristmasFeelings #ChristmasTime*

› *This year, shine with us! Merry Christmas! #ChristmasFeelings #ChristmasTime*

› *Merry Christmas and happy holidays from our family to yours #HappyHolidays #FestiveSeason*

Christmas Decoration

› It's beginning to look a lot like Christmas at *@nameofyourhotel*. Don't forget to share your festive moments with us throughout December by tagging us at *@nameofyourhotel* for a chance to feature on our feed.

‣ Make it Merry! *#Decoration #ChristmasTree #FestiveSeason*

‣ The festive atmosphere is set at *@nameofyourhotel*. Celebrate the Holiday Season at our resort to make the most of this memorable time of the year *#Decoration #FestiveSeason #ChristmasTime*

‣ Festive cheer is already in the air! 🌨️🌲 Celebrate the joys of Christmas with us at *@nameofyourhotel* / *@nameofyouhotelrestaurant* *#Christmas #FestiveSeason #ChristmasDecoration*

‣ *@someone* is loving our Christmas decorations at *@nameofyourhotel*. We send you our warmest holiday wishes and thank you for following our journey since our opening in *(date of opening)* *#ChristmasHolidays #ChristmasWishes*

New Year's Eve and Gala Dinner

‣ Any plans for New Year's Eve? We have prepared for you an unforgettable evening with a Gala dinner, Jazz live music, a magic show and many more surprises *#newyeareveparty #goodbye #galadinner*

‣ Ring in *@completeyear* with us! *#GalaDinner #NewYearsEve*

‣ Join us for a magical Christmas Eve dinner *#NewMenus #ChristmasEveDinner #UniqueDinner*

‣ We are excited to once again host an elegant Christmas Eve Dinner at *@nameofyourhotel* / *@nameofyourhotelrestaurant* *#NewMenus #ChristmasEveDinner #UniqueDinner*

› Thank you to all of our guest who made (@completeyear) an incredible year. We look forward to seeing you on (@completeyear) ! #NewYear #NewBeginnings

Christmas Brunch

› The magic of Christmas is also in our gastronomic proposals. Take pleasure in celebrating Christmas with a festive brunch on December 25. #Brunch #Christmas #ChristmasTime

› This Festive Season, get closer to family and friends with our delicious Christmas Brunch #ChristmasBrunch #Brunch #Christmas

› Start (@completeyear) with our New Year's Brunch, to begin the year in a happy mood! #brunch #newyear #happybeginnings

Christmas Take Away

› Surprise without cooking? This year we have two new menus ready to go! Hurry Up! Takeaway available for December 24 and 25. Please, order by December 20 and pick it up at @nameofyourrestaurant #ChristmasTakeAway #TakeAway #Christmas

› *Christmas menu Take-Away available! We would be honored to take care of the preparations to make your festive days perfect and memorable #ChristmasTakeAway #TakeAway #Christmas*

› *It is only two more weeks to go until Christmas! 🎁🎿 Add a touch of class to your festive celebrations by ordering our take away menu. Please order by December 20 and pick it up at @nameofyourhotel / @nameofyourhotelrestaurant on December 24 and 25 #ChristmasTakeAway #TakeAway #Christmas*

Christmas Repost / Tag Us

› Thank you for sharing your festive moments with us. We're delighted to see you enjoying our hotel this holiday season. Here are some of our favorite images *#BestMoments #Christmas #FestiveSeason*

After Christmas

› New challenges for *(@completeyear)* 👏 Are you ready for our new offer? We are waiting for you! Link in bio *#NewSeason #Challenges #HotelOffer*

› New plans, new adventures and all new destinations to visit during this year! *#HappyHolidays #HappyNewYear*

› Start the New Year right at @nameofyourhotel *#HappyHolidays #HappyNewYear*

Christmas Content Ideas

› **Find a Christmas mascot (Santa Claus, penguin, or elf) and place it at different points of your hotel. You can create a story and a lot of excitement for your future guest.** Example: Christmas comes early! Our *@nameofyourmasctot* have visited soon this year! *#AlmostChristmas #ChristmasTime*

› **Make a video of turning on the lights in your hotel.** Example: Our Christmas lighting is switch-on! 🌟🎄 A joyful tradition in our hotel that begins tonight. Join us! *#FestiveSeason #ChristmasLighting*

› **Put a sled in the hotel and invite people to take a photo and upload it to social networks.** Example: get on our traditional sled and share you Christmas moment at *@nameofyourhotel* with us!

- **Make repost. Ask your guest to tag you with a unique Christmas hashtag.** Example: Don't forget to share your festive moments with us throughout December by tagging us at *@nameofyourhotel* for a chance to feature on our feed.

- **Boost the sales of your gift cards.** Example: there's still time to have your gift card delivered before Christmas Day. Hurry Up! 🌿🎄

- **Record the Christmas decoration process in your hotel with a time-lapse technique.** Example: How are you celebrating the festive season? We're busy adding the extra-special touches to our hotel. 🌿🎄

Christmas Recommend Hashtags

#ChristmasMoment #FestiveSeason #BeautifulChristmasTree #ChristmasTree #FamilyandFriends #Christmas #NewYearsEve #GalaDinner #ChristmasBrunch #ChristmasHotel #ChristmasHotelOffer #ChristmasOffer

SUMMER TIME

Summer Life

› Summer should get a speeding ticket, right? 💨 *#SummerEscape #SummerLife #UniqueSummer*

› Current mood: Eat. Pool. Sleep. Repeat 😉 *#SummerEscape #SummerLife #UniqueSummer*

› Stop scrolling. Paradise found. #SummerEscape *#SummerLife #UniqueSummer*

Ice Cream Time

› Never settle for just one scoop! *#Summer #IceCream #HotelSummer #SummerEscape*

› Every day should start with coffee and end with ice cream *#Summer #IceCream #HotelSummer #SummerEscape*

› It's   ice cream o-clock *#Summer #IceCream #HotelSummer #SummerEscape*

› All you need is ice cream *#Summer #IceCream #HotelSummer #SummerEscape*

› Peace, love, and ice cream *#Summer #IceCream #HotelSummer #SummerEscape*

Cocktails

› Happy National Pineapple Day. Let the celebration begin. *#Cheers #28June #June #Cocktails #HappyNationalPineAppleDay*

› Cheers to pineapple drinks in paradise! *#Cheers #28June #June #Cocktails #HappyNationalPineAppleDay*

› Why drink out of plastic when you can drink out of a pineapple? *#Cheers #28June #June #Cocktails #HappyNationalPineAppleDay*

› Happy National Pineapple Day🍍! Celebrate the day by ordering your favorite cocktail in a fresh pineapple. *#Cheers #28June #June #Cocktails #HappyNationalPineAppleDay*

› If you like Piña Coladas...you know the rest. 🍍 *#Cocktails #TropicalDrinks*

› Who says we can't cheers to a Monday? ...Because that's what being on #vacay is all about! #Cocktails *#TropicalDrinks #Summer #SummerForever*

› Margaritas made me do it! *#Cocktails #Summer #SummerForever*

› Your favorite sips, served fresh at *@nameyouofyourhotelrestaurant #Cocktails #Summer #SummerForever*

› *Sipping paradise on @nameyouofyourhotelrestaurant #Cocktails #Summer*

Swimming Pool

› Another beautiful pool day *#PoolTime #Summer #SummerAtThePool*

- It is just you and the pool 👐 *#PoolTime #Summer #SummerAtThePool*

- Some of the best memories are made in bathing suits *#PoolOpening #Pool #Summer #SummerAtThePool*

- Sorry! Out of office 🤭 *#PoolSide #Summer #SummerLife*

- Taking hanging out to another level *#Relax #Pool #Summer #HotelPool*

- *Get your beach towel ready—Our @nameofyourhotel is calling.*

- *Blue skies and poolside vibes at @nameofyourhotel #Relax #Pool #Summer #HotelPool*

- *Cocktails taste so much better at the pool... but don't just take our word for it #Relax #Pool #Summer #HotelPool*

- Poolside paradise like you've never seen it before... Our pool has officially just reopened its doors! *#Relax #Pool #Summer #HotelPool*

- Making a splash at *@nameofyourhotel #Pool #Summer #HotelPool #BestSummerEver*

- Just chilling with my unicorn *#Unicorn #Pool #Summer #SwimmingPool*

- Never leaving! *#Pool #Summer #SwimmingPool*

- Who wouldn't like to float away on this friendly flamingo? *#Pool #Summer #SwimmingPool #Flamingo*

- It's time for a cool dip! Our hotel swimming pool is now open *#Pool #Summer #SwimmingPool #Hotel*

- The best way to work on a tan? Ideally with a drink in hand *#Pool #Summer #SwimmingPool #Hotel*

- Just another pool day 🍹 join us for a sip and a swim! *#Pool #Summer #SwimmingPool #Hotel*

- At *@nameofyourhotel* everyday is a pool day! Book your getaway now (Link in bio) *#Pool #Summer #SwimmingPool #Hotel*

Vacation Goals

- That feeling you get when your dream vacation has finally arrived. *#DreamVacation #VacationMode #ParadiseFound*

- Monday goals: dip in our lagoon-shaped pool *#DreamVacation #VacationMode #ParadiseFound*

- That summer feeling...*#paradisefound #pool #summerfeelings #pleasures*

- Just another day in paradise! 🌺 Who would you like to sit here with? Tag them *#paradisefound #pool #summerfeelings #pleasures*

Sunset Time

- Catch as many sunsets as you can *#sunsettime #SunsetHotel #Surroundings*

- Just in time for golden hour 🌅 *#sunsettime #SunsetHotel #Surroundings #GoldenHour*

- Cherish every sunset at *@nameofyourhotel* *#sunsettime #SunsetHotel #Surroundings #GoldenHour*

- Sunset Happy Hour at @nameofyourhotel #sunsettime #SunsetHotel #Surroundings #GoldenHour

- Our favorite color is sunset. And yours? #sunsettime #SunsetHotel #Surroundings #GoldenHour

Summer Party

- Spice up your night! We welcome you to host your private summer party at @nameofyourhotel with entertainment, cuisine and decor tailored to you. Link in BIO #Summer #SummerParty #Event #HotelEvent

- We've got the rhythm 🎶 #Summer #SummerParty #Event #HotelEvent

- You will always feel forever young at @nameofyourhotel #SummerParty #Event #HotelEvent

Summer Content Ideas

- **Spend a day with a bartender. Show the process and explain why it is unique.** Example: Your favorite sips, served fresh at @nameyouofyourhotelrestaurant #Cocktails #Summer #SummerForever

- **Propose vacation goals for your guests. You can make a repost of their content.** Example: Monday goals: dip in our lagoon-shaped pool #DreamVacation #VacationMode #ParadiseFound

- **Check sunset time and make an awesome timelapse. Your guests are going to love it.** Example: Collecting unique sunsets at @nameofyourhotel #DreamVacation #VacationMode #ParadiseFound

- **Show real summer life. Try to inspire by showing how is a summer day in your hotel**. Example: That summer feeling… *#paradisefound #pool #summerfeelings #pleasures*

- **Organize a summer party and make a lot of pictures and videos. You will have content to flashback and reminders for a long time**. Example: A flashback to happy tunes at @nameofyourhotel *#SummerForever #Flashback #SummerParty #SummerHotel*

- **Buy a lot of airbeds and ask your guest to tag you in their cool Sumer pics. You will have repost for a long time**. Example: Who wouldn't like to float away on this friendly flamingo? *#Pool #Summer #SwimmingPool #Flamingo*

- **Show summer routines. Inspire people to book. Months before summer you can make creative shots with sun cream, cocktails, towels, or people sunbathing at the pool**. Example: Taking hanging out to another level *#Reading #Summer #SummerHotel #SummerEscape*

Summer Recommend Hashtags

#SummerHotel #SummerEscape #SummerForever #Flashback #SummerParty #paradisefound #pool #summerfeelings #pleasures #Cocktails #SunsetHotel #Surroundings #GoldenHour #DreamVacation #VacationMode #SummerGoals #HotelGoals

VALENTINE'S DAY

Happy Valentine's Day

‣ 🩶 Love makes the world go round. Happy Valentine's Day! *#HappyValentinesDay #Valentines*

‣ When love is in the air...*@nameofyourhotel* replies! Celebrate your most romantic moments with us! *#romantic #loveisintheair #valentines #valentinesdecor*

‣ Our *@nameofyourhotelrestaurant* has turned red! We wish you a nice candlelight dinner. More info in our link in BIO *#HappyValentinesDay #Valentines #loveisintheair #valentines #valentinesdecor*

Romantic Dream Room

‣ Have you booked a romantic night away for your loved one for Valentines? Look no further — we can create your dream room 🩶 *#HappyValentinesDay #Valentines #loveisintheair #valentines #romanticroomhotel #roomhotel*

‣ 🩶 Would you like to make your room extra special? 🩶 Look no further — we can create your dream room 🩶 *#HappyValentinesDay #Valentines #loveisintheair #valentines #romanticroomhotel #roomhotel*

Valentine's Day Offers

› In the most romantic month of the year…indulge in a moment of pure relax with your loved one with a special 20% off! Call our therapists. *#romantic #loveisintheair #valentines #hotelspa*

› Love is in the air at our Spa…can you feel it? Pamper yourself and your loved one with our special «Love is in the air» package on Valentine's Day! Call our Spa Team for bookings or check our link in BIO. *#romantic #loveisintheair #valentines #hotels*

› Treating yourself to a special moment with your loved one. That is our idea of a Valentine's evening at *@nameofyourhotel*. Link in bio for more info. *#romantic #loveisintheair #valentines #hotelspa*

› This Valentines; relax, dine and stay with us. *#romantic #loveisintheair #valentines #hotelspa #hoteldinner*

› Will you be my Valentine? Treat your Valentine to a romantic experience in *@completenameofyourhotel #romantic #loveisintheair #valentines*

Valentine's Day Countdown

› Valentine's Day is coming at *@completenameofyourhotel #Valentines #loveisintheair #valentines*

› With just under 1 month to go until Valentine's Day, it's time to start thinking of how you're going to treat your loved one! Click in our link in BIO and enjoy our Valentine's Day ideas! *#Valentines #loveisintheair #valentines*

› Only one more week to book your valentines day plans! *#Valentines #loveisintheair #valentines #valentineplan*

Valentine's Day Packages

› Valentine's Day Package 🤍 Stay in @yourbestroomhotel + Valentine's Dinner for 2 + breakfast. To book: link in BIO or @completeyouretelephonenumber *#Valentines #loveisintheair #valentines #valentinesdaypackage*

› Setting the scene for a weekend of romance at @nameofyourhotel *#loveisintheair #valentines #valentinesdaypackage*

› Perfect combination of luxury, privacy and a stunning panoramic view to wake up to each morning. Enjoy our weekend of romance at @nameofyourhotel *#loveisintheair #valentines #valentinesdaypackage*

› This is our Valentines Week Special *#loveisintheair #valentinesdaypackage #valentines*

› Nothing says 'I love you' like an overnight stay at the luxurious @completenameofyourhotel *#loveisintheair #valentines #valentinesdaypackage*

Valentine's Day Content Ideas

› **Create a special romantic city break for your hotel. Take pictures in beautiful spots of your city and publish twice a week during January.** Example: Are you ready for our special romantic city break? Link in BIO *#loveisintheair #valentines #valentinesdaypackage*

› **Keep it simple. Grab a rose or other Valentine iconic object and inspire people to book.** Example: Complete your experience by choosing one of our special Valentine's packages: 🤍 *3 nights for the price of 2* 🤍 *#loveisintheair #valentines #valentinesdaypackage*

› **A Valentine's gift always works.** Example: Book now and 🩶 Free room upgrade and a unique complimentary dining experience *#loveisintheair #valentines #valentinesdaypackage*

› **Plan Valentine's Day giveaway in your hotel.** Example: Would you like to spend Valentine's Day with us? Mention your partner. Share the photo in your stories and tag us. Good luck! *#loveisintheair #valentines #valentinesdaygivewaway*

› **Take pictures with a unique Valentine's Day card for your hotel.** Example: Share your love with our special Valentine's Card. Find it in our reception. *#loveisintheair #valentines #valentinesdaycards*

Valentine's Day Recommend Hashtags

#valentinesday #valentienesdaygift #valentinesdaydecor #valentinesdaycards #valentinesdaygoals #valentinesdaytreats #valentinesdaygiveaway #valentinesdayspecial #valentinesdayflowers #valetinesdayiscoming #Valentines #loveisintheair #valentines #valentinesdaydinner

EASTER TIME

....

Happy Easter

‣ Easter is here! A good excuse to eat even more chocolate! *#HappyEaster #Easter #HotelOffer #EasterTime*

‣ Happy Easter from *@nameofyourhotel* 🐣 🎁 We have a gift for you: check in your room and enjoy your sweet surprise 😍 *#HappyEaster #Easter #EasterTime*

‣ Time for some egg hunting ! *#HappyEaster #Easter #EasterTime*

‣ Egg-tivity at *@nameofyourhotel #HappyEaster #Easter #EasterTime*

‣ *Don't forget to enjoy the fun activities this Easter: Egg Hunting, Egg Crafting & Painting #HappyEaster #Easter #EasterTime*

Easter Brunch

‣ Some things are just better in pairs. That is why we celebrate Easter Brunch on *@CompleteDay* and *@CompleteDay* starting at *@CompleteHour #HappyEaster #Easter #HotelOffer #EasterTime*

‣ Be our guest this Easter, and celebrate at a delicious brunch with your loved *#HappyEaster #Easter #HotelOffer #EasterTime #EasterBrunch*

‣ *Someone said Easter Brunch. Join us! #HappyEaster #Easter #HotelOffer #EasterTime #EasterBrunch*

Easter Escape

› Indulge yourself with our special Easter retreat. More info in our link in BIO *#HappyEaster #Easter*

› Make the most of your Easter break with our special package. More info in our link in BIO *#HappyEaster #Easter*

› Easter is just around the corner. Ready for our unique Easter Break? More info in our link in BIO *#HappyEaster #Easter*

› Our Easter Break experience is coming! Ready? More info in our link in BIO *#HappyEaster #Easter*

Easter Content Ideas

› **Look for an Easter mascot and take creative pictures with it around the hotel. Example: Our easter bunny wishes you a Happy Easter!** *#HappyEaster #Easter*

› **Share the feelings of your destination with nice pictures. Inspire people to book your hotel with the Easter moments of your place.** Example: Could be more beautiful @nameofyourcity in Easter? *#EasterTime #HappyEaster #Easter*

› **Spent a few days looking for great brunch easter stock photos. Look at the style and try to take similar photos the day of your brunch. You will have great photos for next year.** Example: Be our guest this Easter, and celebrate at a delicious brunch with your loved *#HappyEaster #Easter #HotelOffer #EasterTime #EasterBrunch*

› **Think about Easter vibes. Try to share this feeling with unique photos.** Example: A great book and a delicious breakfast at the bed. Our Eater escape is around the corner! *#HappyEaster #Easter #HotelOffer #EasterTime*

- **Surprise your guest with egg hunting in your hotel.** Example: Time for some egg hunting! *#HappyEaster #Easter #EasterTime*

Easter Recommend Hashtags

#EasterHotel #Easteroffer #easterbreakfast #easter #eastereggs #easterbunny #easterdecor #easterweekend #easterbreak #easterpackage #easterescape #happyeaster #eastervibes #easterparty #easterbrunch #eastertreats #easterholidays

IT'S HALLOWEEN

Halloween Hotel Offer

‣ No tricks, just treats! Use the offer code *@TREATnameofyourhotel* when booking directly through our website. *#Halloween #HotelOffer #HotelHalloween*

‣ Spooktacular offer! 🎃 Use the offer code *@TREATnameofyourhotel* when booking directly through our website and and receive a 15% discount. *#Halloween #HotelOffer #HotelHalloween*

‣ ‼️🎃Halloween Special Offer‼️ Trick or Treat yourself!👻 Book another night stay and receive a 10% discount using the offer code *@TREATnameofyourhotel.*

‣ *Come stay with us this Halloween weekend! #Halloween #HotelOffer #HotelHalloween*

Halloween Food and Beverage

‣ Save the date for the scariest night of the year! Celebrate Halloween with exclusive new cocktails and a very special DJ set. For more information and to reserve your table please call @completeyournumber or LINK in BIO *#Halloween #HotelOffer #HotelHalloween*

‣ *Boo!* 👻 *You're invited*👻 *Celebrate Halloween at @nameofyourhotel #Halloween #HotelOffer #HotelHalloween*

> *Happy Halloween! We wait for you at @nameofyourhotelbar with our scary Halloween cocktails! #cocktails #Halloween #HotelHalloween*

Halloween Hotel Decoration

> Wishing all our guests a Happy Halloween! Have a fabulous creepy evening…#Halloween #HalloweenDecoration *#Pumpkins #TrickorTreat*

> Halloween is approaching at *@nameofyourhotel* 🎃 *#Halloween #Pumpkins #TrickorTreat #HalloweenDecoration*

> We wish you a spooky and funny Halloween night! Are you going out costumed? *#HalloweenDecoration #Pumpkins #TrickorTreat*

Halloween Content Ideas

> **Create a Halloween offer.** Example: Trick or retreat 🎃 We have a spooktacular offer for any direct booking in October! 👻 Book a 5 - night stay and receive a 15% discount. Use the offer code *@TREATnameofyourhotel* when booking directly through our website.

> **Create a unique event and share a lot of pictures after Halloween.** Example: Kids can carve a pumpkin for FREE if you book a table on Friday 30th or Saturday 31st October!

> **Ask your chef and take pictures with a unique Halloween dessert in your hotel.** Example: Any child who has Lunch or Dinner at *@nameofyourhotel* in fancy dress this Halloween can enjoy FREE dessert!

> **Talk with the reception for Halloween. They can dress up and create a special welcome for your guest. It's a great day to create**

unique content. Example: our reception team wishes a Happy Halloween! #HotelHalloween *#Halloween #Reception*

> **Create storytelling with a Halloween mascot around your hotel.** Example: our skeleton Jack is ready for Halloween at *@Nameofyourhotel.* And you?

> **Talk with housekeeping and get ready to take awesome pictures of Halloween photos of your hotel.** It could be really useful for next year. Example: Halloween is approaching at @Nameofyourhotel 🎃 *#Halloween #Pumpkins #TrickorTreat #HalloweenDecoration*

Halloween Recommend Hashtags

#Halloween #HalloweenHotel #HalloweenHotelOffer #HotelOffer #HalloweenDecor #HalloweenParty #Halloweencustomes #Halloweeneveryday #halloweenspirit #halloweenlife #halloweenlover #halloweenideas #halloweenchallenge #halloweencountdown

MOTHER'S DAY

Happy Mother's Day

▸ Happy Mother's Day! *#hotel #mum #mothersday*

▸ Wishing all the Mothers out there a truly Special Happy Mothers Day. *#hotel #mum #mothers day*

▸ We hope that all Mums out there get the special day you deserve and have a Happy Mother's Day *#hotel #mum #mothersday*

▸ Treat your mum at with these five fabulous Mother's Day ideas. More info in our link in BIO *#hotel #mum #mothersday #mothersdayideas*

▸ The unique Mother's Day hotel break is here! More info in our link in BIO *#hotel #mum #mothersday #mothersdayideas*

Mother's Day Stay Package

▸ Pamper the mothers and special women in your life with an indulgent stay at *@nameofyourhotel* *#Mothersdaypackage #hoteloffer #MothersDay*

▸ Treat the special lady to a Mother's Day she won't forget at *@nameofyourhotel #Mothersdaypackage #hoteloffer #MothersDay*

Gift Cards

▸ Just say thanks mum! With a @nameofyourhotel gift card *#hoteloffer #MothersDay #giftcardhotel*

- *Mum, you rocks ! Giveaway a @nameofyourhotel gift card #hoteloffer #MothersDay #giftcardhotel*

Mother's Day Lunch

- Lucky mums! Join us in our special lunch and receives a complimentary bottle of wine! #MothersDay

- *Enjoy our Mother's Day lunch and receives a 25% off in our spa treatments. You deserve it! #MothersDay*

Mother's Day Content Ideas

- **Show in a video how is a Mother's day escape in your hotel.** Example: That is how mums enjoying our Mother's Day Escape. Ready? *#hotel #mum #mothersday*

- **Take lifestyle pictures of your mum enjoying a spa massage or a dinner.** Example: Current mode: best mum escape forever! *#hotel #mum #mothersday*

- **Grab a hotel gift card and take pictures around your hotel in great spots.** Example: Just say thanks, mum! With a @nameofyourhotel gift card *#hoteloffer #MothersDay #giftcardhotel*

- **Wish happy mother's Day. You don't need a model. Try to look for something representative. It could a flower or a nice card with a quote.** Example: Wishing all the Mothers out there a truly Special Happy Mothers Day. *#hotel #mum #mothersday #MothersDay #happymothersday*

- **Show Mother's day vibes and ideas.** Example: Promise. Best mum breakfast hotel is ready! #hotel #mum #mothersday #MothersDay #happymothersday

Mother's Day Recommend Hashtags

#mothersday #happymothersday #mothersdaygift #mothersdaygiftideas #mothersdaycard #mothersdayvibes #mothersdaygoals #mothersdayweekend #mothersdayescape #mothersdayspecial #mothersdayflowers

FATHER'S DAY

....

Special Lunch or Dinner

› We have plenty of treats to make Dad feel special at *@nameofyourhotel* Link in BIO for more details *#FathersDay #FatherHoliday #FathersDayHotel*

› Get ready to celebrate Dad with lots of love, incredible food and live music. Link in BIO for more information *#FathersDayHotel #FathersDayOffer*

› Join us at *@nameofyourhotel* this Father's Day for Lunch or Dinner. There will be a Special Father's Day Menu. Link in BIO. *#FatherHoliday #FathersDayHotel #FathersDayOffer*

› "The best way to a man's heart is through his stomach". Fathers deserve to be pampered too, give us a call and celebrate Father's Day with our special menu at *@nameofyouthotelrestaurant #FatherHoliday #FathersDayHotel #FathersDayOffer*

Father's Day Hotel Package

› Make it a special day for Dad at *@nameofyourhotel* with a Father's Day package for only *@completeprice #FathersDay #FatherHoliday #FathersDayHotel #FathersDayOffer*

› Looking for Father's Day trip ideas? Click our link in BIO to read about these great destinations and treat dad to a weekend getaway this year! *#FatherHoliday #FathersDayHotel #FathersDayOffer*

- Find the best gift for your Dad at *@nameofyourhotel* and put a smile on his face this Father's Day. Our unique offer is in our link in BIO *#FatherHoliday #FathersDayHotel #FathersDayOffer #FathersDay*

- *@nameofyourhotel* is hosting a very special Father's Day. Join us! *#FatherHoliday #FathersDayHotel #FathersDayOffer*

- Treat the special super hero in your life at *@nameofyourhotel* *#FatherHoliday #FathersDayHotel #FathersDayOffer*

Father Gift Card

- This Father's Day, treat your dad to a signature experience with our Gift Cards *#FatherHoliday #FathersDayHotel #FathersDayOffer #GiftCard*

- Our Father's day gift voucher is a very nice gift for your dad! Check all details in our link in BIO *#FatherHoliday #FathersDayHotel #FathersDayOffer #GiftCard*

- We have some of the very best Father's Day gift voucher ideas in *@nameofyourhotel #FatherHoliday #FathersDayHotel #FathersDayOffer #GiftCard*

- Happy Father's Day! Being a dad is one of the best experiences you can have in life. *#FatherHoliday #FathersDayHotel #GiftCard*

Father's Day Content Ideas

- **Ask your dad for a photo session at your hotel. Take pictures at the spa or enjoying a meal. It would be great for your marketing efforts.** Example: Nothing better than a spa day at *@nameofyourhotel* for the best dad ever! *#SpaDay #fathersdayhotel #Fathersdayspecial #fathersdayideas*

- **Make a list of different Father's Day treats and inspire your guest.** Example: Coffee, newspaper and all morning at the bed. Yes, it's my special day and I deserve it! #fathersdayhotel #Fathersdayspecial #fathersdaytreats

- **Create a Father's Day Contest in your hotel.** Example: Participate and win a night at @nameofyourhotel for your Dad! It's our turn to make him gibe some time for himself! How to participate: Follow us! Mention your Dad in this post. Share this post on your story and tag us. Good luck!

- **Make a unique video on how it could be a Father's Day Weekend in your hotel.** Example: That is how our Dad's enjoying a Father's Day Weekend #fathersdayhotel #Fathersdayspecial #fathersdaytreats

- **A special gift for your guest. It could be a chocolate or card with a discount at the restaurant. Make someone special that day. You can create storytelling for Father's Day with an action like that.** Example. If you are awesome dad. An awesome gift awaits in your hotel room. Check it out! #fathersdayhotel #Fathersdayspecial #fathersdaytreats

- **Explain with lifestyle pictures how it is your unique Father's Day Offer.** Example. Make it a special day for Dad at @nameofyourhotel with a Father's Day package for only @completeprice #FathersDay #FatherHoliday #FathersDayHotel #FathersDayOffer

Father's Day Recommend Hashtags

#FatherHoliday #FathersDayHotel #FathersDayOffer #FathersDay #Fathersdaygifts #FathersDayWeekend #FathersDayGiveAway #FathersDayQuotes #FathersDaySpecial #Fathersdayideas #Fathersdaycontest #fathersdaypresent #fathersdaytreats

HOW TO CREATE BETTER CAPTIONS

Find Your Target Audience First

You have to have in mind for who are you writing. Does my audience like long or short captions? Shall I need to use emojis? If yes, what emojis will my audience like? Is my message clear enough?

Read a Lot

Try to read more. It is important to know more about different writing styles. Also, you have to improve your vocabulary and looking for proper spelling, grammar and punctuation.

Choose Your Tone of Voice

Don't copy. Be creative. Inspire in others but keep your own style. According to the tool sociality.io:

"Depending on the niche, you might need to be funny, serious, neutral, or emotional. Identify your brand voice in accordance with your niche.Of course, it also depends on the content you share, but generally, if you have a specified tone of voice, your audience becomes aware that it's your brand's way of expressing your thoughts, and they get comfortable with it".

Buy a Notebook and Keep It Always With You

Buy a notebook and keep it always with you. You never know when it is going to appear inspiration. Keep in mind your topics and try to be short and direct. Try to say more with fewer words.

Planning Is the Key

If you want to have success and get more bookings in your hotel, you have to plan everything. Think about your goals and produce content in line with it.

Hashtag Research

Did you have a hashtag strategy? It is not about copy hashtags and copy. It is about the performance of the hashtag and your chances of appearing on the top. Try to use the tools recommended in this book and think first.

Hotel hashtags

Topic-related hashtags

Destination hashtags

Check Your Competitors' Posts and Engagement

Check a competitor on Instagram are not about copy all the captions. It is a great option to define your strategy and know more about what is working on Instagram.

Short or Long Captions?

Our recommendation is better short than long. However, it depends on your brand strategy. According to the tool sociality.io:

"If your post is longer than 125 characters, your followers will have to click 'More' to read the whole caption. If three lines are enough to highlight the importance of the post, then you are good, no need to add more than that. After all, it is not easy to express a whole idea with limited characters. However, if your thoughts are longer than 125 characters, don't hesitate to write them in a long but organized way. Remember that spacing, having paragraphs, and relevant emojis will be visually pleasing for your audience as they will easily find the information they are looking for."

Write a Killer First Line

People don't read. Try to say the most important in the first lines of your caption.

Don't Forget To Add a Call-To-Action

It could be the price of your hotel offer, link in BIO, telephone number, or book now. A good CTA can inspire your followers to engage with your business website, sign up for a newsletter, or book your hotel.

Keep Your Instagram Captions Clean

We are totally agree with the tool later.com when they said that: *"Adding hashtags to your Instagram caption is a great way to make your posts more discoverable, but too many hashtags can make your captions look untidy.*

Equally, adding hashtags too soon in your caption can encourage users to click away from your post — which is the opposite of what you want to achieve!"

For more information

BIBLIOGRAPHY

....

› <u>SOCIALITY.IO. E-Book. How to write good Instagram captions</u>

› <u>LATER.COM</u>

    <u>The ultimate guide to writing good Instagram captions</u>

    <u>Instagram caption length</u>